W9-BZG-385

PICK ME AN APPLE!

by Shelley Rotner

SCHOLASTIC INC.
New York Toronto London Auckland Sydney
Mexico City New Delhi Hong Kong Buenos Aires

*To the apple
of my eye.
—S.R.*

*Apple pie recipe used by permission
of the Black Dog Tavern Company,
Vineyard Haven, MA.*

ISBN 0-439-39554-2

12 11 10 9 8 7 6 5 4 3 2 1   2 3 4 5 6 7/0

Printed in the U.S.A.

First printing, September 2002

Do you like to eat apples?

Yes, we do!

There are so many kinds
of apples to enjoy —
yellow, green, or red,
sour or sweet,

Macintosh,

Fuji,

Granny Smith,
and more!

Apples are fruits
that grow on trees.

During the winter,
the apple tree rests.
The buds on the
branches are protected
from the cold by
a hairy covering.

The buds stay dormant, or inactive,
through winter.

Inside each bud are all the leaves and flower parts that will grow on the tree throughout the entire year.

In spring, the buds begin to open,
and soon the tree is covered with
new green leaves.

Then the flower buds start to grow, and
the green, leaflike flower pushes through.

As the days become warm and long,
the flowers develop. Each blossom
has five petals that are either pink
or white.

Soon the flowers fade, and the petals
fall to the ground.

The fertilized apple flower remains and starts to
grow into an apple.

The stem delivers food and water to help
the apple get bigger.

Throughout the summer, the apple tree is covered with green apples.

By the end of the summer, the apples are almost full grown. The weight of the apples bends the branches downward.

In autumn, the days get cool, the temperature
drops, and the apples begin to ripen.
Most apples now turn red.

But there are some varieties that stay green or change to yellow.

When the apple is fully ripened, it's ready to pick!

If you cut an apple in half, you'll see five seeds inside its core, or hard center.

Around the core is the tasty white part of
the fruit that you eat.

Now it's time to take a big bite out of that juicy apple!

What's
your
favorite
kind
of apple
to eat?

APPLE PIE

from the Black Dog Bakery Café, Vineyard Haven, MA

Make sure to ask for a grown-up's help before you start making this tasty treat.

Crust:

2 cups all-purpose flour
1 teaspoon salt
3/4 cup vegetable shortening
4–5 tablespoons ice water

1. Combine flour and salt in a medium bowl.

2. Use a pastry blender or two table knives to cut the shortening into the flour until the shortening-flour mixture looks like large rice grains.

3. Sprinkle dough with ice water while blending with a fork until the dough is just moist enough to hold together.

4. Cut in half. Shape each half into a smooth ball. Protect with plastic wrap. Then refrigerate until ready to use.

Filling:

6 Granny Smith apples
1 teaspoon ground cinnamon
1 teaspoon ground nutmeg
1/2 cup sugar

1. Peel, core, and slice the apples into thick wedges.

2. Then mix and toss with cinnamon, nutmeg, and sugar.

Finishing:

1/2 cup milk
2 tablespoons coarse sugar

Assembly:

1. Flour the rolling pin and surface. Flatten one dough ball by pressing and rolling from the center of the dough out to the edges to make a circle bigger than the pie pan.

2. Slide spatula under the dough and gently lift into the pie pan.

3. Gently trim off any excess dough.

4. Put apple filling in pie shell.

5. Roll out the other dough ball to make the upper crust. Lay upper crust on pie. Or make a lattice design on top of the pie by cutting the crust into 1-inch-wide strips after rolling out the dough. Then lay strips on top of pie.

6. Use the prongs of a fork to press upper crust down around the pie to attach it to the bottom shell.

7. Brush upper crust with milk and sprinkle lightly with coarse sugar.

8. Bake the pie in a 450° oven for 10 minutes, then reduce the heat to 350° and bake for approximately 50 minutes.

9. Serve warm with a generous scoop of vanilla ice cream.

Apple Facts

Did you know?

People have been eating apples for more than 2 million years.

There are thousands of different types of apples.

Some apple trees can grow 35 feet tall. That's twice as tall as the average giraffe!

Apple cider was the national drink of the United States until 1850.

Johnny Appleseed was a real person. His real name was John Chapman.

October is National Apple Month.

Apples can be stored in a cold refrigerator for up to 12 months.